Published By Thought Catalog Books Division
Thought & Expression LLC Williamsburg, Brooklyn
www.thought.is

Founded in 2010, THOUGHT CATALOG is owned
and operated by The Thought & Expression LLC, an
experimental media group based in Williamsburg,
Brooklyn. THOUGHT CATALOG BOOKS is our
book imprint, where we publish fiction and
non-fiction from emerging and established writers
across all genres.

Learn more about our organization and explore our
library at thoughtcatalog.com/books.

Want us to publish your book? Email us the
manuscript for review:
manuscripts@thoughtcatalog.com.

Cover and interior design by Athletics NYC
Cover Photo: © iStockPhoto.com/j0sefino

THOUGHT
CATALOG
Books

The Truth About Everything

By **Brianna Wiest**

For Ally

Table of Contents

INTRODUCTION

THIS BOOK IS A compilation of work that was written at different periods of my life, inspired by different events, but all somehow found its way to Thought Catalog's homepage. There are ideas here that are windows into very personal parts of my life, and I give them to you because I hope that in some way, you can relate. Whatever advice I have been able to give has only been because of the authors and teachers I have studied and learned from. So for what they have given me, I would like to say thank you, and to note that if any ideas or concepts that I have relayed here go unaccredited, I did not do so intentionally, but rather these ideas have had such an impact on me that they are essentially a part of my own thinking and ideology.

When doing writing of this nature, I try to be honest, be vulnerable, give it all I've got and hope that I can ease someone else as the words of others far greater than I have eased me. I have written many things that are deeply personal and I still wince at the thought of other people reading and knowing so much about me. But I do so because I sincerely hope you regard this, and my work in general, as a place to come when your soul needs soothing, something to remind you that your experiences are universal, that you are not alone, and that when things look the most hopeless, you are usually not far from a breakthrough.

I would also like to give a huge thank you to a few people: to Chris and my other talented co-workers at Thought Catalog, thank you for the opportunity at hand. I am forever grateful. For those who have helped me on my own personal and spiritual journey and for those who have not; for those who have loved me but especially for those who have not: thank you. All of the pieces somehow fit together at the end of the day and I wouldn't be who or where I am without what I have experienced. Of course, for my family, friends who are like family (hi, Ally!) and readers: thank you for always coming back and hearing what I have to say. I do not claim to know it all, but I just want to give you what I have and hope that it helps you in whatever way you need your life to be helped right now. Happy reading.

THE CATACLYSMAL AND INCONSEQUENTIAL

IF YOU'VE NEVER REALIZED how small you are, you should stop to think about the reality of your existence. The universe is vast and cataclysmal and you are an inconsequential speck in the span of it. And yet, you are still an integral and necessary being without whose presence the world would not be how it is. Isn't that in itself miraculous?

Our finite brains can't comprehend the enormity of the state we live in, let alone the universe in which we reside. A universe that is just as alive as we are. A universe that, somehow, we still control and effect. Because as much as life is an illusion, it is also poignant and remarkable. You are given what you need. There is a greater force at work that we theorize about but can't quite definitely understand. And maybe that's just how it needs to be. Because if everything were explained, there would be nothing left to figure out. There would be no journey or development or growth. We are all essentially still in a childlike state when you consider what we know compared to the knowledge of the universe. But we lose the wonder.

We lose the wonder because we are gutted by our lives. We are literally and metaphorically cut open, killed and left to either resurrect ourselves or sit in that nothingness. What compels me to believe in humanity, and what keeps me in love with people, is that most often, we choose the former.

You do have love. It's surrounding you and it's brought you here. It's so easy to forget where you are when you stare at the same four walls day-in-and-day-out. You can feel as though your part-time job waiting tables yields no consequence. But all while you're distracted by the mundane and the ordinary, the miraculous surrounds you, you're just blind to it.

There are stars colliding and life is evolving and things are transforming and existence is coming and going, it is, always will, and has been even in the 5 seconds it just took you to read that sentence. Whenever you feel hopeless, all you need to do is go outside and realize that you have been molded into human form for some reason. You are somewhere you may never be again. Your actions, no matter how inconsequential you think they may be, have been essential.

Pain is part of the process. It's part of the miraculousness. You see it when light shines through storm clouds, in the refracting lights of supernovas, in the fact that you must be in a physical state to comprehend the physical things around you–sight, sound, material. But it is also those senses that facilitate your pain. All of these things are rooted in suffering, and yet they all yield the miraculous. So be here. Be part of what you're sewn into. Bloom where you're planted. Be aware of the greatness that you are and realize that without you, the seaming of this mysteriously interconnected world would cease to exist as it is. Hope is never gone, it's just ignored.

YOU ARE MY HOME

I REMEMBER THE FIRST time I heard your voice. I can still remember telling you how soothing I found it, how much it calmed me. It still does, even though we're strangers. You're silent, but your words are still very much alive in me. You are my home, even though the door is locked and the lights are off.

It's not a choice as much as it is a beautiful nagging that's nearly impossible to ignore. But I'm locked out, left to wander, and I've found myself here. I know I left in a childish fit, and you locked the iron gate so tightly; you had to. So I was left out in the darkness, just me and the shadows that haunted me, the ones that led me away from you to begin with. You left me outside to face them. You wouldn't let me lean on you to deal with them anymore.

You are my home because you are the place I choose to return to over and over again. The place that, even when painful, means the most. You are my home because you have made me who I am, whether or not you realized what you were doing. You are my home because you showed me the best kind of love there is.

You showed me real, genuine, love-you-so-much-it-hurts-and-changes-me-at-my-core love. It was a blissful combination of finally feeling alive mixed with the most painfully difficult challenge I never thought I'd have to deal with. I didn't know I could ever feel so strongly that I'd end up there.

And yet, I still believe, that although that love may have been all of those challenging things, it was still unconditional, undeniable, and above all, beautiful. Miraculous. And that's what keeps me at your door.

I've found that, at the end of the day, what's hurt me the most has been thinking I wasn't loved by the people I found myself inextricably bound to. In some cases, it was a biological attachment. But in our case, it was something that goes beyond that.

It's as though the longing for acceptance from the people we are most devoted to, body or soul, is the most painful thing when not reciprocated, and yet, we care so much it can haunt us for our whole lives, if we let it. I wanted to let you know that the shadows in my life have been replaced. You exorcised them and your memory resides instead.

ON BEING A CREATOR

I'VE HEARD THE IDEA phrased and presented in a hundred different ways, but somehow, in one way or another, I keep crossing paths with the same message, and it's that we are the creators of our own existence, every part of it. To some it's free will, to others it's the Law of Attraction. I've never put it in such terms, but I have researched these ideas just out of interest. I'm no expert by any means, but I just want to relay some of what I've learned that has resonated with me.

Some people really believe that if you visualize what you want, you can manifest it in your life. To a degree, I've found this to be true. When I wholeheartedly intend to do something, I end up, one way or another, doing it. It's not to say that there's no difficulty, or that there's no challenge to do it. It's just that when I've decided that I am something, or that I will do something, and I have unfailing faith that my affirmation is the truth, it comes to fruition in one way or another. Coincidence? Maybe. But its this simple process that has sparked my interest in the idea of our roles as creators.

I used to firmly believe in fate, and I suppose I still do. But that belief, for me, used to imply that our lives were somehow out of our control. "It's just fate," I'd tell myself. "What's meant to be, is meant to be." And although I do believe there is some greater orchestration and intricate plan that was devised for us (or by us) pre-incarnation to aide us in our soul development, I think we can choose how we experience it. A very wise friend once explained it to me this way: If you're meant to go from point A to point B, you will get there, eventually. But you can choose which way you go, and how you travel.

I guess another way to think of it is that the vibrational frequency at which we function will be the reality we live in. That's not as much of a religious doctrine or teaching as it is a scientifically-rooted idea. Every bit of matter is made up of vibrating particles. This idea has helped me to make sense of how we are all connected, and one with the Earth. Look at a leaf close up, you'll notice that there are veins in the leaf that look just like ours do. Look at a map, and you'll see that the riverways look just like our veins do as well. We're all one, and in my opinion, the idea that we're separate from anything is merely an illusion of consciousness. Therefore, by that logic, wouldn't we have to assume that the ideas we conjure in our heads are also created externally?

It's the Buddhist teaching that "what you think you will become," and that there is no way to happiness, because happiness is the way. It's the teaching that you should have unwavering faith in God, and it's the idea that good things happen to good people, karma. I've been hearing this message since I was a little girl, even in my favorite Disney movie: "no matter how your heart is grieving, if you keep on believing, the dream that you wish will come true."

Today I went to my local used bookstore and bought about six books, a few having to do with these ideas that I've found myself fascinated by recently. As I sat down to read them, I realized that the introduction to one of the books that I bought was written by the author of another one of the books, and the introduction of that book was written by another author that I had also purchased. I randomly chose these books from random places in the small, used bookstore. They were obscure books and authors I had never heard of before. It wasn't as though I was buying a collection of books that would obviously have similarities. Normally, I'd think to myself, oh, that's such a weird coincidence! But in the context of what I was looking to read up on, I couldn't help but feel as though I was, so to say, "attracting" these things to me.

I don't think these ideas are applicable to only one religion or belief system. I think even if you don't believe in the idea of God, you can still consider the idea of vibration, energy and frequency, and how our minds create for us. The way it's made the most sense to me so far is that how did we get here from where we were a year ago? We thought up what we should do next, and we went for it. We arrived. It's as simple as that. Tomorrow, you've decided (or will decide) what you're going to do, and thus you are the creator of all that happens. I don't know about you, but there's something absolutely thrilling to me about being the creator of my existence, the writer of my story and the artist of my masterpiece, and I will forever be looking to prove this idea true with my own life.

THE REVOLUTIONARY AND UNDEFINABLE

THE DAY MY GREAT-AUNT died, my mom and I went to visit her, as we often did after school. She was pretty much bat-shit nuts in the best way possible, and she had cared for me everyday since I was six weeks old, while my mom went to work. She suffered a series of strokes that eventually left her half-paralyzed, incoherent and wired up for life support in a nursing home.

I remember as I rested my hand on her arm that day, it felt cold. We called a nurse to check her vitals, but she said everything was fine. Unsuspecting, we left. We left her in that room, her only company the little trinkets and gifts we brought for our own peace of mind, really. Just in case one day she woke up, she would know that she was loved. That last time I left her room, as I was almost out the door, I turned around and said, "I love you." She died a few hours later. That was the last thing anyone ever said to her. How extraordinarily lucky I felt, to be able to have given her her last words. And how lucky that they happened to be "I love you."

A year or so later, my little brother was born. The first time I held him, I told him I loved him. I loved that little person who I didn't even know yet. I loved him just because he was alive. He redefined what I knew love to be, much like my great-aunt did.

I used to think it was just a feeling, but I learned it was also a verb. I thought it was an expression of gratitude for someone who had done something for you, but I realized that it didn't have to be. You could love someone unconditionally. When I went to college and met my first serious boyfriend, love was redefined for me yet again. It's been constantly revolutionizing for me, in ways I didn't know possible until they happen.

So after all this time, seeing some of the infinitely undefinable and differing kinds of love, wondering to myself what the hell it all even means, I realized that it means whatever you want it to. You don't have to find someone who fits a certain set of standards that you had in your head for when you'll fall in love with them. Sometimes, it just happens. Sometimes it's not love, and you think its, but you discover otherwise. That's okay, because love is whatever you make it out to be. Love is undefinable because it's constantly being redefined. To the best you're able, make your last words "I love you" and all the rest of them proclamations of that love... so you have someone to say it for you, if you're unable.

WE BUILD OUR OWN CAGES

WE BUILD OUR OWN cages and live within them because we think they will keep us safe. It's like building a wall around our hearts. Some of us are internal about it but I think in many ways that safety net is legitimate and physical. I think we see something that threatens our being, confidence, any sense of knowing that we're okay — and we set up a bar. We know to not go there again. But when we start living within that cage, and decorating its steel bars with pretty little flowers, we're brainwashed into thinking that it's the real, free universe. That's the stuff of breakdowns. We stop building cages and start digging graves.

It's like the fear of someone or something or somewhere just penetrates our psyche and we're following that dictator like we have no mind of our own. Some call it irrationality. To the extent that we're able, we decide when we're going to allow ourselves to be free, when the dictator is our own fear. We must free our minds. Even the caged bird can sing, if only he can find the tune.

I remember when I let my own world come crashing down on top of me. There was no cathedral to protect me, God did not reach down his hand and help me up. Scared, and defeated, I laid there and reached, begged, pleaded, that he wouldn't let this happen. I had to break and shatter the idea that anything could be changed unless I changed it. Are there miracles? Sure. But at the very least, you'll never even see it happening if you don't get up and look.

Free yourself from the confines that bind you. Maybe you built steel bars around your heart because you thought they had to be there. You wanted to protect yourself from being hurt so badly again. Take them down. Walk out. This may be physical or it may be metaphorical. But either way, know that there's nothing worse than not experiencing life for the fear of what it may bring.

YOUR PERSPECTIVE IS EVERYTHING

I ONCE HEARD SOMEONE say that in writing, and in life, there's only one story-line, and it's that nothing is ever as it seems. Sometimes I wonder if this is because everything is malleable. Everything is someone's perspective of it, most often your own. No two people see everything the same way, so how is there anything definitive, when it's all a matter of perspective?

It's the root of fear vs. hope, failure vs. triumph, and so on. Because what is failure other than our own assertions that we've failed? And where do those assertions even come from? The ideas of other people? Because their ideas are just perspectives too.

What I guess I'm trying to say is that perspective is, and always has been, the only truth that there is. Take, for example, when you're learning about history. You're learning from a textbook, that had to have been derived from historical documents, that were documented by people who presented their own perspective, because that's what they experienced. Even if that did consist of acknowledging someone else's ideas, that's still under the umbrella of that person's perspective. We learn about the American Revolution in a different way from how people in England learn about it.

And maybe this is something that can be used to our greatest advantage. If life is just a matter of perspective, can't that instantly instill hope for every situation we're in?

Because even though something may seem like a gut-wrenching tragedy, that may only be our take on it. With a grain of salt and keeping things in perspective, it's the idea that nothing is ever as good (or as bad) as it seems, because it can seem differently, based on how you look.

I like to think of success as being the measure of living up to your own goals and expectations, aka, your perspective on what's best. If you consider a different perspective for success, you may not see yourself as a failure after all.

And maybe that's the beauty of falling in love; with anyone, anything, anywhere. Somehow, that person (thing or experience) reached inside and made you see the world differently. The most miraculous things in our lives are the ones that change how we see things, each other and ourselves. It's the relinquishing that hope is not lost, for there is another way that life can be.

Although it's not to discredit people's feelings, and how very real and very painful some experiences can be. Your perspective is valid, and real, and you are allowed to feel however you feel about what's happening in your life. It's not to say that just looking at it from another point of view will be an instant fix for your troubles. It may just, for the lack of a better phrase, put into perspective that life is subjective, temporary and fleeting, sometimes terribly painful but also extraordinarily beautiful... all at the same time.

THE CRACKS IN LIFE LET THE LIGHT THROUGH

REALIZING THAT I WOULDN'T be who I am nor would I be able to do what I love most without having the cracks in the pavement on my journey is probably the best realization I've had as of late. I realized I've learned to stop brushing off criticism and start listening to it. Because even if some people are cruel, I can get past that, and listen in case something they are saying is rooted in the truth. When I stumble, I look at what it is I'm tripping over. Not doing so may be one of the greatest mistakes.

And what I've noticed about myself is that the things that bother me most are the things that are the most true. So I listen when it hurts. I personally try to consider a perspective I may have not seen before. I try to learn and grow and be better. Because if I realize that it's honestly the truth, then it's something that I have to honestly come to terms with. The more I've been able to do that, the happier I've become. I don't see criticism as daunting anymore. I've been able to look at struggles and challenges and those days where I'm just plain old fed up and miserable as passing segments of my life. Temporary moments that make way for the light to come through. If I hadn't known suffering, loss, sadness and all the other crap life slaps out, I wouldn't be a writer, because I wouldn't have anything to write about. If I had a perfect life, I would never have had the chance to hurt but then to grow and experience more, feel more, be more. I like to think of pain as my heart just stretching out.

And the point is, that's what works for me, but what works for you may be much different. Nobody's light is going to be exactly the same, but it's important that you do find it.

A professor of mine once shared a personal story of how, after finishing her undergraduate degree, she struggled to find work and had to move back in with her parents. At the time, she thought it was the worst thing ever, and she was overcome with grief and feeling as though she had failed. Not even two weeks after she moved back home, her father died suddenly. After he died, she was accepted into the graduate school she wanted to go to and went forth to pursue her education and eventually found her way. She said that she couldn't be more grateful for that time she had at home, because it was the last time she got to spend with her dad. She did not pose this story to us as any kind of proof of religion or God or why we should believe. She was just saying that this is what she experienced, and ever since, she has had unfailing faith that everything does literally happen for a reason.

I can't help but concur. The light came through the cracks of her life, and I'm sure it's coming through yours as well... it just may not be time to see it yet.

ACCEPTANCE IS TOMORROW, IN A SMALL, QUIET ROOM

AN AUTHOR WHOM I very much admire, Cheryl Strayed, once said: "Acceptance is a small, quiet room." I've found myself in that room, realizing that there's no grandiose parade to arrive there. There's no welcoming committee or celebration that you've finally made it. Nope, none of that. It's just you, and the quiet, almost silent (if even there at all) realization that you've turned to a new page of your life.

It's the step forward you don't realize you're taking until you're on the other side. It starts when your lover tells you it's time to move on and accept that you'll never be together again. It's that first moment, that cutting, gut-wrenching moment, when you realize you're being told to move on by the person you have to move on from, a person who has clearly already done so, that can impale you to rock bottom.

And while you're laying there, at rock bottom, there's something you realize. When you have to accept and move on, it's because there are no other options to exhaust. You'll never answer the questions that linger in your mind because there are no answers at this point. There is no way to make that person love you again, or to go back and undo your actions. There is no other answer when your only choice is acceptance. There's also no way to rid yourself of your feelings if they're there. So what is there left to do when you're so desperate to move forth but so compelled to hold on by your emotions? In that first moment of humbling pain, you begin to think of moving on as a place to get to. You think of acceptance as another element that will be present in your life–that you desperately need to be present in your life. But really, acceptance is just allowing yourself to move to the next thing: the next lover, the next job, the next whatever-it-may- be, because there is nothing that will release you from your thoughts other than having new thoughts to fill your mind. It doesn't mean the pain will instantly dissipate, but nothing will facilitate the dissipation more than changing your life will.

It's when you can look back and say, hey, I may not be okay with the fact that that happened, and I may not ever be, but there are new things in my mind and heart. New things to take my energy and attention. Things that actually deserve it. Things that don't force me into having to accept anything I don't want to or move on. Acceptance is tomorrow. Even if the pain is still there, you realize it may always be, and somehow, that's okay.

Regardless of the feelings that linger, if you have no other options, tomorrow, acceptance is where you need to be. Accept the new things that come into your life, or put new things in your life, if you need to. Tomorrow can be your small quiet room, you just have to take a step in there.

THE 10 DECISIONS THAT CHANGE YOUR LIFE

1. **Deciding that you have the power to change.** I'm all about the power of thought and the fact that we're all creators of our own experience. The day you decide you want to change something about your life is the first step of the journey.

2. **When you choose to make your work what you're passionate about.** The bills have to be paid and you have to get dinner on the table somehow, I know. But if there's anything you decide to do, please

make your life work what you love to do most. You don't have a career, you have a life. Live it.

3. **When you make your own family.** You decide who that consists of: biological family members, men, women, friends, spouses, lovers, kids, animals, whoever. Family is one of those things that I believe you can choose. And there are few things more important than your family. Whoever you choose them to be.

4. **When you start living within your means.** In many cases, not all, it's just a simple issue of people who aren't living within the means they earn. This does not apply to people living in poverty, obviously.

5. **When you discover the simple things that make you happy, and make it a**

point to do them every day. I've always been taught that we have a base line level of happiness that we eventually revert to, regardless of what joy or sorrow we experience intermittently. The best way to change your life is to change the little daily routine things, the things that will up your base line of happiness.

6. **When you choose to give your time and energy to others, and not just yourself.** There is something unspeakably rewarding about servicing others. It tends to give your life a new sense of purpose, your being a reason other than just for itself.

7. **When you work toward embracing what you can't change.** It will be a struggle, there's no easy way to

accomplish this. But imagine what could be if you took little steps toward doing so.

8. **When you take the time to just stop and enjoy the moment you're in.** Isn't it always about the next greatest thing that you'll be happy once you have? Consider what you have now that you thought you'd be happy once you got.

9. **When you love who you actually love.** I know it's a simple observation, but one day it just hit me that people aren't always together because they love each other. There are a thousand different reasons people get (and stay) together and some of them can be the farthest thing from love. If this is your truth, change it. Go love who you actually love. If you don't know **first step in changing.**

Change won't who that is yet, keep living, they will come.

10. **When you know you want a change, because it's the** happen until it's initiated by the self, and for the self. When you realize you want to have a better life, you are acknowledging your own self-worth.

IF YOU WANT EXTRAORDINARY LOVE, YOU NEED TO FIGHT FOR IT

THE TIDES OF LIFE won't always bring you back ashore — sometimes, you have to row yourself over. Often, nothing changes until you change it. Nothing is better until you make it that way. There's nothing you're not responsible for. Just waiting around for something to happen, lamenting that it isn't, wishing, hoping, praying for it to change, doesn't always ensure that it will. Go, move, act, speak. Your days are slipping by you, and every day you spend in the mediocre is another you miss in the extraordinary.

If you're seeking the miraculous, keep seeking. Life is unimaginably short and passes even faster than that; there will be enough average things in your life. Don't let love be one of them. Because if it's unconditional, life-changing, mind-altering, madly- passionate-sometimes-extraordinarily-difficult-but-none-the-less-just-plain-extraordinary love that you find yourself inherently invested in with every bit of your heart, if it's the person who is there beneath the layers of your heart that you've calloused over through the years — you need to go be with that person. Be with who uproots you and makes you realize you didn't know how deeply your soul could stretch. Be with who loves you. Who really, actually, genuinely, truly, madly, deeply, passionately loves you. And to whom you reciprocate the feelings to as well.

This does not mean be with the person that you most easily get along with. Sometimes, extraordinary love isn't easy (it usually never is) but in one way or another, it is always worth it. So don't mistake the extraordinary for what you're settling for. I know this is an extremely difficult thing to do most times, because when there's nothing really wrong with your relationship there's no reason to wreak havoc and go...except, there is. And that's because the extraordinary is waiting for you somewhere else. In the words of Cheryl Strayed, *have the courage to break your own heart.* That's awesome if you really like each other, and even if everything is swell but yet, somewhere you know, this person doesn't absolutely rock your world, you need to go.

Because you need (and deserve) love that is something of an other-worldly connection, that you can't really make sense of in your mind. Mind-blowing-life-changing-heart-stopping-blood-rushing-miraculous love. Don't settle until you have it, if that's what you want.

There is no time for love that isn't miraculous. Get up and leave. Move. Go. Don't hold on because you think you'll never find someone else. If you're even a little bit unsure, leave. Your uncertainty should tell you that at the very least, you need to explore other avenues. And if those roads lead you back, great. If they don't, great. Wanting to leave is enough reason to go. And believe me, one way or another, you will eventually wind up where you're supposed to. Whether it's with some cool new person or back into the arms of the person you left, you won't ever have to question whether or not you should be with them.

AN OPEN LETTER TO MY FELLOW HUMANS

Dear Everybody,

This is the letter I wish someone would write to me. Rather, these are the things I have to keep reminding myself, and some of the many things that I most genuinely want you to know, especially if you ever find yourself in doubt.

You are not fat. What does "fat" even mean, anyway? Where is the gauge on whether or not you're fat? I care less about the fact that you have extra weight on your body than I do of the fact that you spend your time worrying about it. It's not to say you should be unhealthy; as long as you're taking care of yourself, you're more than just okay — you're beautiful. You're not too shrimpy or strangely shaped or whatever it is you think you have too much of or lack on your body. Find the parts of you that are much more important, relevant and genuine than how you look (looks will fade over time, hope that's not news to anybody). You will be loved more for this. Be the awesome, caring, fun-to-be-with people you are, and the people who should be in your life will love you for that.

What is going to matter in a month, year, decade from now? Probably not many of the stupid, little, irrational, nonsensical things you're plaguing your mind with. Don't waste your time if it's not going to be something honestly worth putting your energy toward. This too shall pass. There are two ways I look at each day, and it's that your pain and suffering is temporary, but at the same time, that the wondrous things in your life will pass as well, so enjoy them while you can.

Please remember, and yes I'm about to quote Coldplay, that *the sun must set to rise.* Sit and think about that. Not everything can be wonderful at all times because nothing in your life would change. You'd never move on to the next thing. And even if that seems appealing, you need to move on to experience more, find more, be more. Find whatever it is that makes your soul swoon and be that, do that, live that. Be who you are. Listen to your instincts. That little voice that is often drowned out by the rest of your thoughts: stop and listen. You'll find your way.

The way to stop hate is to stop hating. Be better. Never stop seeking the extraordinary. Never fail to forget your role as a creator of your own life. You choose tomorrow, and you create what is. Make sure it's what you want. Be happy. I love you. Find other people that love you as well. Be with them.

THE THINGS I WISH SOMEONE WOULD HAVE TOLD ME

WHEN I THINK OF the things I wish I knew five years ago, I'm wrought with both shame for having been so immature and naïve, and yet also inspiration, seeing how far I've come.

Some of the things I wish I knew back then are probably the things I am going to wish I were more conscious of in five years from now.

I wish I knew that a "normal" life isn't so definitive. I was so afraid of just being average, ordinary. I wish someone could have explained to me what I was actually afraid of: not living my life before it passed me by. I wish I knew that the only real measure of success and normalcy is your own gauge of it. I wish someone would have told me to calm down and enjoy where I was, because I'd miss it eventually. I wish someone would have told me that the things I would remember in a few years from now are not how concerned I was about my weight (which was nothing to be concerned about, by the way) or how disappointed I was in myself. I wouldn't remember the days I spent loathing and lamenting, but I would remember the key moments that defined that period in my life.

Not the thousands of moments I spent unnecessarily upset.

I wish I knew that what I would remember as the good times were the point where I didn't care about anything other than enjoying myself. I still remember a specific period of time where I honestly accepted myself, and did what I wanted because I wanted to. The rest of the time I spent I worried that I wasn't good enough. Good enough for my friends, whether or not I had real friends, good enough for the college I wanted to go to, for my parents, for anybody to ever love me.

I had opened the door and was taking the first steps down into what would become the darkest period of my life. 5 years ago was the first point where I should have seen the warning signs and done something. I wish someone would have told me that it's okay to get help. It's okay to do something. It's okay to think you're worthy enough to have a beautiful life. I wish someone would have told me I was worthy.

I wish someone would have told me all the things I could, and would, become. I wish someone would have said to me, Brianna, you are more than just "good enough." You know all the great things that you're capable of. You just have to get up and do them. I wish someone would have told me that the "someone" I wished would tell me these things was myself. Because more than anything, I wish that someone would have told me that the only person I was looking to please was me. I was the problem and I was the answer all along. I don't know how it took so many years and so many different people to figure out.

YOUR SUBCONSCIOUS IS CONTROLLING YOUR LIFE

YOU HAVE YOUR THINKING mind and your subconscious mind. The best way I've heard the latter described is that it's like a tape player, a computer, a processor, replaying whatever you program it to. It's not the subconscious mind that's evil or negative. It's what you've formatted it to do that can wreak havoc–even if you didn't intend to "program" it a certain way. Your subconscious is what's running the show. It's the driving force behind your functioning biology, and it's what's responsible for your instinctive feelings and reactions that may not always initially make sense. It's a million times more powerful than your conscious mind. So in a sense, your subconscious is controlling your mind.

It's our mistake to think that when things don't work out, we're victims of something external. If our intentions were for wonderful things, how can it be our fault when things go wrong? Well, it's because your subconscious is running the show, regardless of what conscious thoughts you're sifting through. We sabotage our own lives with behaviors that don't support our subconscious. It's not too different than saying we should listen to our instincts.

"Matter derives from mind; mind does not derive from matter." It's just another of the dozens of ways that we can confirm how we are creators of our own experiences, of our own lives. It's the law of attraction. It's positive thinking. It's fate. It's gut feelings. You've heard it presented and theorized in so many different ways.

The universe is made of energy: this, we know. But before we knew that, we kind of had to pawn the unknown on faith and religion. We had to have faith in what was happening around us, in the invisible moving forces that influenced our physical lives. Another way that's described is as being the "field" of the universe. Both science and religion are defining the same truth.

HOW SLEEP PARALYSIS LED TO MY CURRENT RELIGIOUS BELIEFS

I SHOULD START BY explaining that I was born and raised a Roman Catholic. It was during my teenage years, in which I was still a devout Catholic, that I had the experiences that led me here. I'm sure whatever force has guided me thus far will continue to do so, and I may be back one day with a whole new understanding of things — and I hope that day does come to pass. Until then, here's what I've got.

I was lying in my bed in my parent's house, I was probably about 16. I had just started to doze off to sleep when I felt my body start to vibrate and I heard a humming in my ears. I couldn't move. I was awake, but my body was asleep. At the time, I thought I was having a seizure because of the incessant vibrating. (I realize now that I probably wouldn't have been conscious if I were having a seizure.) Anyway, it was in that moment, when my body was "asleep" and my consciousness was awake, that I could literally, physically feel the separation of my body from my soul. I had understood the idea of having a soul within a temporary physical, human body, but never like this. These episodes continued. To this day, they were the most uncomfortable experiences I have ever had. I saw all the necessary doctors, only to have them all agree that what was happening to me was much less serious than a seizure — it was just sleep paralysis: where your body paralyzes itself for sleep, but your consciousness doesn't go "off" at the same time. A fairly common issue, they claimed.

I'm not sure that these basic, human words can really explain how I grew to understand from these instances, but it was something like this: I knew that my body was temporary, and that I was in this for the experience, for my soul to develop. I understood that the world was an illusion of consciousness, created, again, for our development. It wasn't so much that I was taught these things as I just understood from, literally, feeling my soul. For me, religious ideas began to make sense. I started to look at the overlapping, continuous beliefs and teachings that spanned through all of the religions, not just the one I was raised in. I began to see how my faith taught me to personify a lot of ideas so that they were more easily accessible and understandable for me. I also saw that that method didn't resonate with me as much as another could.

I questioned how I could be taught that there was an all-knowing, all-loving, wonderful God who loved us all equally, no matter what we did, and yet, there was so much suffering and unfairness in the world, and that at the end of this journey, we would have a judgment day. I wanted my God to be judgment-free. Wouldn't he have to be, to love me entirely?

But I reformed this, and I'm not saying any of the prior ideas were (or are) wrong. Religion is subjective and it's however you can best connect with your inner spirituality. I believe you should be able to choose your religion, because at the end of the day, there's only one truth that's there. But there are a hundred different ways to be taught, and to understand, and to access that truth. You have to find the one that works for you. For me, it's knowing that God is just the force of love, and all other wonderful things in the world.

Because I don't call myself a Catholic anymore, I am sometimes called an atheist. This couldn't be further from the truth. I know that I am a piece of God, and that I decide my faith and my fate. My state of consciousness determines where I go next, "judgment day." There are many lives and experiences that I will have, all for the sake of the development of my soul. There is a plan that God has for me, and it's intertwined with the truth that I'm living now. I was able to find my religion through my own experiences, and I encourage everyone else to do so as well. If something doesn't make sense for you, or doesn't resonate in the right way, you must dig, and work through it, and get to a place of understanding. If a religion where mysteries are an integral part of the faith doesn't work for you, find your own path. Even if that means scoping a whole new one out for yourself.

WHY YOU CAN'T LET GO

YOU KNOW WHAT YOU'RE holding onto. I know what I am. And I also know that there are many others that have, are, or will be, holding onto something as well. Sometimes it's for a minute and sometimes it can last for years. Regardless, it's debilitating. It's paralyzing. It keeps you stuck in what could have been.

After we seek all the advice we can, it usually rounds out to the same thing: it's time to let go and move on. If you're anything like me, just reading that sentence made your heart sink a little and you're filling up with resistance, shame and anger. You don't want to let go. You want to hold on until you're right. You want to hold on until the situation resolves itself the way you want it to.

Because what's the alternative? You have to go on without that person or thing that you thought you'd never be able to live without. But can I tell you something? You're living without them right now. Life has moved on. That person or thing has as well. And you're still here. You're still functioning. Life didn't wait for you to catch up, and it never will. Holding on will not make something come back. In my experience, it actually pushes it farther away. You cannot go back and undo what's done, my friends. You can only move forward. And if your deepest compulsions and instincts tell you that you're meant to be with that person or doing that thing, you should let go and move forth and see how life takes you there. Clearly, things aren't going according to your desired plan already, so why not throw caution to the wind and see where you end up.

And something else to remember is that the things that eventually work out are usually infinitely better than what we had to let go of. I'm sure you can see that in your own experiences. And even if you are brought back to where you hoped you would be, the path was lined with something you had to learn. There aren't many accidents. In fact, I'd like to argue that there aren't any at all. If you don't want to take my word for it, think back on an instance where you were in the throes of depression or anxiety, and couldn't understand how or why your life was turning out the way it was. How did that situation turn out? Probably fine. Because that's where we all eventually end up.

Life is not a series of problems to be solved, it's a journey that you should be fascinated by. Sit back and observe as you live. Signs and directions and messages are everywhere, if you only pay attention. Follow them, they know where you're going. To hell with logic. Love isn't logical, nor are miracles. You can't let go because you're worried that if you do, what you're so desperately hoping for will fall apart. I have news for you. You're tearing it down yourself. Make way for the bigger, the better, the reckoning, the miraculous and the beautiful. It's ready for you when you are.

PEACE IS IMPERFECT ACCEPTANCE

AS I LOOK DOWN at my "coexist" bracelet, I'm finding myself thinking why and how wearing this silly hippie bracelet makes any damn difference in the world. I know it's there to remind me to accept others unconditionally, but other than that, what's the purpose? If you've ever wondered what real, attainable peace is in the world we're living in, join the club. It seems like we're all seeking the trifecta: peace, love and truth. But how can it even be possible when so much of our existence is characterized by the heartbreak and misfortune that surrounds us?

And what even is peace? Is it just non-violence? No killing, no wars waged, no physical, literal negativity? I'm not sure. Because peacefulness is so much more than the lack of violence. It's harmony. It's contentment. It's the merging and coexisting of a thousand different people without conflict. It looks pretty close to impossible.

We're never going to be flawlessly peaceful human beings. We will always be wrought with the anxieties, depression, insecurity and pain that our ancestors have. It's the human condition. But I suppose what we can do is learn to not take those difficulties and project them onto other people. We can't tell other people how to live.

Even if it's wrong. Even if we inherently disagree with it. Even if every fiber of our bodies and souls are screaming that we should just slap some sense into someone, we have to let them go through their own process. Because as adamantly as we believe that they're wrong, they believe that they're right.

I've said this a dozen times and I'll say it again: peace for the world around us has to begin within us. Individual changes in consciousness are what will propel the world into peace, love and truth. Forcing other people to follow suit will not further your cause. You have to lead by example. Change your own level of consciousness and watch how others follow by their own volition.

What does changing your consciousness mean? It means opening yourself and accepting challenges as nothing more than mere turning points and lessons. Seeing negative criticism as someone's failed attempt at possibly telling you something important: they just didn't know how to say it kindly. It is listening to what's negative, and being with it, not running from it. It's reaching, and loving and knowing that there is more than where you are right now.

It's understanding what matters, and knowing that those things are not what most people think. It's not reaching a place where there is no pain, it's just learning to love through it. It's where we can have our differences but talk through them and find a solution that's not violent or pain-staking. It's acceptance of what isn't meant for us. It's learning to not resist the way life leads us, knowing and believing that there are greater plans intact. It's you and me stepping down from lashing out just once, and letting that wave tide over us and recess.

7 QUESTIONS THAT TELL YOU WHO YOU ARE

MANY OF THE ANSWERS we're seeking are answers we already have. We just don't know how to access them. Understanding who you are isn't something you stumble upon one day. It's embedded within you; you just have to be vulnerable long enough to uncover it. Your everyday actions are shouting what you may not be conscious of.

1. **What would you do with your life if you didn't have to pay the bills?** If money weren't an issue, what would you do with your days? Would you write?

75

Read? Sing? Whatever it is, you have to do that thing. Money is an interesting phenomenon that completely controls our everyday lives without having any purpose other than sustainability in the form of purchasing from others what we could produce and create right in our own backyards. Consider that when you're deciding between a soulless job that will make you rich versus a life that will feed your passions.

2. **What cuts you the deepest?** So much is defined by what we're most affected by. Really, what do you not even want to think about right now because it brings you so much emotion? Let those things in, and sit with them. Consider them. Integrate them in your life. We call this acceptance. It doesn't mean you have to like it, it just

means it is something that moves you very deeply for some reason, so you shouldn't ignore it. Figure out what that reason is.

3. **If you were going to die tomorrow, what would you do today?** I'd write. I'd sit outside, go for a walk or hike, and write. I'd write letters to my family. I'd probably write articles or ideas for articles. I try (and usually do) those things every day regardless. Not because I have to, or because a writing career is what's going to best pay off my student loans. But because it's what I want to do most. It's who I really am.

4. **Who do you love and why do you love them?** The first people that come to mind are very much a part of who you are. But what's even more important is why you

love these people. Where is your love and what is it based on?

5. **What do you quote?** I'm always interested by what people quote, especially on social media, because really, they're not bringing your attention to something that someone wise said as much as they are trying to tell you something about themselves. Look at what you want to perpetuate to other people, when you yourself can't find the words. What strikes you most is who you are.

6. **In those rare but life-changing moments, how do you act?** When you're at the end of your rope and you have to make a decision, which way do you choose? Notice the patterns in the paths you choose to take. Notice how you help others when they ask for it. Notice

more how you help when they don't. Your instinctive, intuitive reactions do say something about you. I know some would argue that instincts are just by-products of technically being animals, but our instincts are also formed by the thoughts that we craft in our minds.

7. **What do you think about most?** It's the little things that add up and create who you are, and if you really want to see where you're at, write down the things you think about most. They are where you are most invested. They are where you are most curious, interested, perplexed, pained and inspired. These are the things and people who most tell you who you are, because they are the things and people who have remained with you, even if they're not physically there anymore

LIVE OUT YOUR TRUTH

IF YOU KNEW HOW desperately I've been grappling with this lately, you'd probably call me up and make plans to sit me down for coffee and promptly smack some sense into me. You'd probably say, but Brianna, you tell everybody else to do these things, and for some reason, you can't yourself. You're a hypocrite. To that, I would say: yup.

A friend of mine put it to me this way: in every other aspect of my life, I can live out my truth pretty well. When it comes to my love life, I more or less cower like a dog with its tail between its legs. I don't know why I can't just live out what I know is true. My favorite author, Cheryl Strayed, claims that to be how you're most honest with yourself.

I couldn't agree more. I know what I have to do, and I know what the right thing is to do, but dear God I am so afraid to take the leap. Living out your truth means utter vulnerability. You are acting on what is most deeply embedded inside of you. To have people not accept these things, or to be rejected for these things, it's just devastating. But you know what else is devastating? Living a life you don't really want to because you never had the guts to live your truth. What I mean by "your truth" is what you know to be what you most want to do. The person (or people!) you most want to love. The things that cut you open and ignite your nerves and can send you over the edge but you keep going back because you know, despite everything, that this is what's meant for you.

If nothing else, the reason to do it is this: the truth inside you will win out eventually. Or it will drive you mad. Your truth isn't a passing thought or feeling that will just dissipate one day. You won't get over what's really meant for you. You will only ever become more and more aware that you're denying yourself the greatest joy in fear of the possibly greatest disappointment. I can't believe I'm throwing this quote in here, but I can't think of anything that sums it up better: "the brave may not live forever, but the cautious don't live at all."

FATE IS AN ACT OF YOUR OWN VOLITION

I WONDER IF AFTER I die, I'll be able to see my life with clarity. I don't know how my consciousness will manifest outside of a physical, human body, but speaking in the senses that I now understand, I wonder how I'll be able to see my experiences. I also wonder if I'll see them in comparison to what they could have been. I want to see my sister lives, I guess. The lives I didn't live because I chose otherwise. The things I missed, and the things I avoided. The things I managed to free myself from.

I know there is some majestic higher power, and I know that in conjunction with this higher power, I have decided a route for myself. I know there are end-goals and things I need to learn, parts of me that I have to develop, things I have to experience. But I also know that there are different ways to get there, be there and experience.

The lives we didn't choose can haunt us. Most commonly in the forms of guilt and regret. They're the envisioning of everything that could have been, if only we had let them be. But rarely do we look back on the things that we could have had to suffer through if we hadn't chosen otherwise. More often, we acknowledge how life directed us (even despite our most adamant refusal) so we could avoid hardship. We sometimes don't take responsibility for the things we've changed, because at the time, they may have seemed like the obvious choice. Other times, some greater force that has guided us thus far took over. We sometimes call this fate.

Today someone told me to picture my life at 40. I did. Most of it, I liked. There were parts I didn't. I sat for a few minutes, worrying about these aspects of my future life, and a realization hit me across the face. I have to change these things now. This is the life I'm going to live if I stay on the same path. I can change. I will change. I do choose otherwise. That life I pictured today will be a ghost that I forget about because I'll have more important things happening. Why? Because fate is an act of your own volition.

HOW TO ACCEPT WHAT YOU CAN'T CHANGE

1. **Start with moving toward accepting who you are.** If you do some analyzing, you'll find that most problems are, one way or another, rooted in not accepting and loving yourself. This is the best place to start.

2. **Don't rely on ineffective coping mechanisms, find healthy outlets for yourself.** For example, suppressing your feelings and ignoring the problem will never bode well for you in the long term, and you know this.

3. **Make lists, write things out, consider the possibilities.** This is how I deal with mostly everything I can't figure out immediately. I write things down, make lists and weigh pros and cons. For the sake of acceptance, write down why you can't change it or the reasons why you may be happy this happened in the future.

4. **Don't try to change everything at once.** You won't do anything thoroughly if you try to uproot your whole life one day. Take it one step at a time, the best changes, and the ones that last, are the ones that happen in gradual steps.

5. **Find your happy place.** My happy place is often my bed. This is not a sexual innuendo. I just love to nap, read or write while sitting in bed. Your happy place can

be a state of mind or a room in your house. It doesn't have to be some intangible unrealistic place that you won't be able to go to on a daily basis. Find it, and go there.

6. **Find other thoughts to fill your head.** You won't just stop thinking about what hurts unless you find other things to think about. Suppressing your thoughts, as mentioned before, will not make them go away. They'll make them more powerful when they eventually all come back to haunt you. Find new things to think about. Go to bed reading poetry and wake up letting any negative thoughts pass by you and finding beautiful ones to fill your emptiness.

7. **Let the feelings wave through you and pass.** Breathe through them. Don't

resist them, just let them go. You will never, ever, reach a day where you don't have feelings, the good and the bad. Resisting them will not help, it will hurt. Train yourself to acknowledge your feelings, consider what they're trying to tell you, and let them pass.

THE GRACE WITH WHICH YOU ACCEPT WHAT'S NOT MEANT FOR YOU

UNREST DERIVES LARGELY FROM that which we don't have the grace to accept isn't for us. I can think of so many incidents in my own life in which I've struggled only because I couldn't accept what was innately meant (and not meant) for me. Easier said than done, I know. But the things we leave behind are never as wonderful as those that we eventually find. The path is long and unknown but we continue because we know it's also one of growth and experience. The most beautiful things arise from the least promising situations… light can only shine in the darkness, right? To have the grace to accept what isn't meant for you is cultivated by finding hope, trust and faith that you will find greater things, bigger loves and better days. Knowing that when things least look like they're going to change, that's usually when they do.

It's like there's some extraneous force that can see beyond what you can and can guide you to better things. This is your God, parent and best friend. Finding trust in it is grace. The things you cannot change are the things you'd want to change if you had them. Doesn't seem like it now, but trust me. The universe has the best understanding of what's meant for us — especially when we don't.

There's a famous Christian parable that I feel applies well to this idea. Please note that I do not affiliate myself with Christianity, so

I would like to use this just as text to be analyzed.

One night a man had a dream. he dreamed that he was walking along the beach with the Lord. Across the sky flashed scenes from his life. For each scene, he noticed two sets of footprints in the sand; one belonged to him, and the other to the Lord. When he looked back at the footprints, he noticed that many times there was only one set of footprints. He also noticed that it happened at the lowest and saddest times in his life. This really bothered him and he questioned the Lord about it. "Lord, you said that once I decided to follow you, you'd walk with me all the way. But I have noticed that during the most troublesome times in my life, there is only one set of footprints. I don't understand why when I needed you most you would leave me." The Lord replied, "During your times of trial and suffering, when you only see one set of footprints, was when I carried you." This, I believe, is human-projection of the idea that when it least seems the universe is on your side, it's most guiding you and carrying you. It aligns with my overarching belief that the common themes throughout religion and spirituality in general are the things we should most note. That is how I've built my own spirituality and I think that even if you decide to practice one definitive religion, it's still important to consider the ideas and principles of others.

I digress. The point is, this idea of a universe that knows more than we do and guides us when we most feel that we are alone is an idea that has been discussed and perpetuated for years. I hope that you consider this within the context of your own struggles. This too shall pass, my friends.

THE THINGS HAPPY PEOPLE KNOW

HAPPY PEOPLE KNOW THAT everything is fleeting. They know that the struggles they face will pass, but at the same time, they also know that the great things that are in their lives will pass as well. Happy people live in the moment.

Happy people don't call themselves "happy people" or think of themselves that way. They define happiness as a sense of peacefulness and contentment mixed with pursuing their deepest passions. This is what happy people know.

They know that few things matter more than how much you love everyone, starting with yourself. They know that loving yourself means respecting yourself and doing for yourself what will make you the best you possible.

They know that nothing should be taken too seriously, and that all they give will be returned to them twofold. They know that there is a greater plan and a higher force. They live in awe and wonder of the universe, and try to maintain a sense of childlike wonder.

Happy people choose happiness because they choose to do what will best facilitate it. If they're struggling with depression, they choose to get help from a professional, or whatever else they may need to get through it. They choose to help themselves, to be brave, and to accept things they can't change, even when it seems most impossible. Because more than anything, happy people know that happiness is never sedentary. They acknowledge all of their emotions and are equally grateful to experience them all. Happy people immerse themselves in the physical life they have now, knowing it's not permanent.

And they all started their journeys as broken people, whether they self-destructed or had unfortunate circumstances or life events come upon them. I know, because I am one of these self-destructing people turned happy. Happy people know suffering more than anyone else, and that's how they can see just how damn beautiful their lives are. It's because they've seen the depths.

HAPPINESS IS TO GENERATE ENTHUSIASM AND IGNITE CURIOSITY

HAPPINESS, IN MY OPINION, is making your mind a more interesting place to live in. It does not mean eternal joy, because that is simply not realistic and if joy were constant it would become the norm and therefore we would be desensitized to it. Happiness is to generate enthusiasm and ignite curiosity.

Happiness is the desire to continue to experience. The times in my life when I am the most happy are when I am interested in something (living a passion) and I'm so engrossed in how this passion intrigues me that my other concerns seem to fall to the wayside.

I'm not saying this makes happiness more attainable, but I am saying that it makes it attainable. Our lives will never be constant, steady or predictable. Joy will come and go, as will sorrow and suffering. What makes all of it worthwhile is feeling as though you have a purpose and discovering that which compels your mind and soul.

I also believe that an element of happiness is acceptance of what you cannot change, but I don't think it's as pertinent as interest is. This, I believe, because there will always be something new to accept. There will always be something you are dissatisfied with, disappointed by or suffering from. This will not cease. Acceptance, while very important, will not solely bring you happiness, although it will bring peace, which is a crucial factor. Acceptance in combination with interest will.

What is love if not just interest, fascination, enthusiasm and the desire to continue an experience with someone? It is not a sustained sense of joy, although joyousness is a part of the experience of love. And when people say you have to love yourself, it means just that: be interested in what you're doing, be enthusiastic for what you will do and desire to continue the experience that you're having.

NOBODY ELSE CAN HEAL YOU

I'M NOT SAYING YOU have to have it all seamlessly together to be loved. I actually think that real love grows when someone finds unspeakable beauty in the place you've been cut open. But the thing is, you can't expect someone else to heal those wounds. They can love you and that love can facilitate healing, but you are the only person who can heal yourself. Nobody else will ever be able to alleviate your burdens. It may seem like it for a little while, but the brokenness of your foundation will always show eventually.

Yes, love is transformative and enlightening and humbling and probably the most real thing we can experience. It is responsible for a whole slew of miraculousness, but romantic love will not solve your problems. The high you get from the newness of someone will eventually subside, as it always does, and you'll be left even more raw than you were before, facing the brutal reality that the thing you were waiting for to fix everything didn't.

It's for this reason that I believe we often see people undergoing self-transformations after breakups. Of course there are other reasons for these behaviors, but I do think that in many cases, it has to do with people realizing that nobody else is responsible for resolving their own issues.

I know many couples who have found one another and rely on each other to function. They are the epitome of unhealthy, and what they all have in common is that they all found their partners while they were honestly broken people. For example, a friend of mine found her boyfriend while she was coming off of an addiction to hard drugs, and had honestly lost her will to live. She never healed from those experiences, she just learned to lean on her boyfriend and to this day, she still says that if he ever left her, she would kill herself. She's not exaggerating.

People and love can be the most integral part of the healing process. But you can't just wait for somebody else to do the work. You have to get your ass on the floor, realize that you're imperfect and you feel unworthy and you've made mistakes and you're afraid of this and that and the other thing. You have to come to terms with these things that are inside you. You don't have to like them. You just have to be able to sit with them. You have to be okay enough to still be standing on your own if and when somebody leaves you there.

The happily ever after will not save you, and the love of your life will not heal you. They will only love you, and while that may facilitate great healing, it can also be the source of your demise if things don't work out until the day you die of old age. If your peace and acceptance is contingent on someone else, and if your hope is external, you do not really have any of those things. Don't fool yourself into thinking you do, it will be a price that you alone will have to pay.

A LITTLE SALT IN YOUR WOUNDS HEALS THEM

WHEN I WAS LITTLE, my mom would take me to the beach while we had summer vacation (she was a teacher, and we lived on Long Island). I remember her telling me to run into the ocean so the salt water would heal the bug bites that I had scratched open, and I didn't want to, because it would make them burn and sting. It's something that's become metaphoric now that I'm older. A few days ago, I called my mom, and as she was telling me about the part of our house that's being rebuilt after Sandy destroyed it, for some reason, I just remembered that a little salt in your wounds heals them.

A little (metaphorical) push is usually what has made me move when I didn't otherwise feel compelled to. Regardless of what great things it yielded, it was still a push, and I hated it at the time. The thing about people is that we don't change unless not changing becomes the less comfortable option. It's unfortunate, but we're creatures of habit and we'll hold onto our convictions until we're literally forced to stop. In retrospect, I would not change much of anything about my experiences over the past few years. I just wish I knew that the salt in my wounds was healing them. I just couldn't see how pain could be growth, healing and reckoning.

Something that I tell myself often when I'm all knotted up inside is that what I'm feeling I will eventually regard as the pain that comes with my soul stretching to be more and understand more and love more... growing pains. Don't run away from the things that will fix you and heal you. They're often unlikely, unexpected and uncomfortable. That doesn't make them bad. It just makes them new. And if you've been around the block enough, you'll know that they always lead to the bigger, better and more beautiful.

25 THINGS LOVE DOES

1. Makes people willing to put even the most coveted things at stake.

2. Unifies through the only commonality needed to understand one another.

3. Creates an inner warmth and willingness to be loving and kind to others.

4. Makes every one of life's hardships and tragedies seem worth it.

5. Provides a sense of purpose.

6. Compels so deeply you'd risk or give your life.

7. Makes the coy outspoken and the outgoing coy.

8. Reforms the jaded and hopeless.

9. Puts people in touch with their true selves.

10. Accepts without condition.

11. Embraces what is, and people as they are.

12. Is unwavering with compassion and forgiveness.

13. Is willing to let go if need be.

14. Connects people of all races and creeds.

15. Unites countries and peoples otherwise war-torn and separate.

16. Uncovers what's most true.

17. Makes people completely reform their ideas of what is "attractive."

18. Either provides convincing evidence of a higher being or at least of the concept of fate.

19. Closes personal distance.

20. Takes down otherwise unbreakable walls.

21. Keeps people coming back to the thing that either has or has the potential to destroy them.

22. Seems to change people, but really just unveils their true selves.

23. Inspires and unfolds.

24. Makes you just mad enough to devote your entire life to another person.

25. Makes way for peace: sometimes with oneself, sometimes with others, but most often, with all the uncertainties that come with life.

14 WAYS TO RETHINK THE LOVE IN YOUR LIFE

1. **Your feelings are not an all-or-nothing-deal.** You can love someone just a little. You can love a lot of people just a little. There's no switch that goes on for every single person you meet that will tell you whether or not you will love them for all of eternity. Sometimes it's a mystery to uncover, and that is a process that should be enjoyed. You will not always be certain that someone is either your soulmate or just a friend, because not everybody falls into either of those categories; there is a

spectrum when it comes to love, and there will be many people in your life who fall along all different ends of it. Love is not an all-or-nothing deal.

2. **The heart and mind should work in tandem.** Love is not logical, but at the same time, you can't just let your feelings run rampant and allow you to make irresponsible, harmful or dangerous decisions, like staying with an abusive partner. It is a tricky equilibrium, but it's important to learn how to listen to your heart first while still considering what your head has to say about it.

3. **It will probably never be defined, so don't try to identify it by making a list and checking off if someone makes you feel a certain way.** Love is to be experienced. You do not love someone

just because they fit into a set of pre-established criteria that you thought would be necessary to have feelings for someone. As aforementioned, you have to let your heart navigate and your head copilot for a little logic and reasoning now and again.

4. **Fulfilling love is not just romantic.** Love is also the essence of who we are. You are not unloved because you don't have a romantic or sexual partner. I have many loves in my life, all of which make me equally happy. I found this on my way to work today, and as I'm sitting here writing this, I'm here to tell you, this is another way that love can be experienced.

5. **Sex and love are different, but are great when they coincide.** Just because someone wants a sexual relationship with

you, or vice versa, it does not necessarily provide much indication of where they are at emotionally. You can have fulfilling sexual relations with people you don't love, and likewise, you can be very much in love with someone without being sexually compatible.

6. **Likewise, marriage and love are different, but are also great when they coincide.** I feel like people expect that if they marry someone it will confirm that they are in love and will be forever because they are legally bound to be. Marriage is not a grand and glamorous exclamation of love everyday of your life. It's paying bills and taking trips to Costco and cleaning up after each other when you're sick and unable. Some people consider that love, and others consider it

obligation. Realize that "happily ever after" is not necessarily marriage, and you have to consider the realities of life post-nuptials.

7. **It is something you do, not just something you feel.** It's a verb. You can have feelings that you define as love, but you do not "love someone" until you act on that, and put them before yourself: their happiness, wellbeing, etc. You should apply this to the people who claim they love you but don't act like it. Words mean next to nothing unless they are backed with action.

8. **It is easily and often confused for lust.** It's hard to differentiate between feelings, since they're usually all bundled up and packaged into one little body that can't make sense of things. But love and lust are

different in one key respect: love puts the other first, lust puts the self first.

9. **There is no end-all-be-all when it comes to choosing a partner.** You can have a fulfilling life with many different people. There are, however, some people who will do more for you than others, this is just the reality of being alive. It doesn't mean, however, that you've lost out on love for the rest of your life because it didn't work out with one person, nor does it mean that you'll never love someone that way again.

10. **It grows with time, it is not stagnant.** It's sometimes easy to think that facing challenges means that your love is depleting, but really, if you want to work through those issues with someone, and you come out on the other side stronger

both individually and as a couple, you've got something good goin' on.

11. **It will change you, if it hasn't already.** Love is not something you blindly experience and then come out of the same. It is transformative. If you're having trouble identifying whether something is love or not, something to consider is the effect it has had on you. I'm not saying that love is selfish and solely about what it does for you, but rather when you love someone with all that you've got, and you let it reverberate through you and impact you completely, you will come out a different person... or more aware of who you really are.

12. **It is not always certain and definite.** You are allowed to be unsure. I think sometimes people get more upset about

not knowing than the fact that they don't know. Embrace the uncertainty and see it as part of the journey... try to understand why you are uncertain, and what matters so much to you that you are considering how other options could pan out better. More than anything, though, realize that there is no "right" and "wrong" necessarily, the universe will autocorrect, just be ready for the plunge.

13. **It is very rarely smooth and flawless.** It is more often all messed up because real love impacts you at every level and brings forth everything you need to deal with. The real fairy tales are what happens when you find someone who changes you and you're able to live happily ever after with yourself.

14. **It can not, should not, and never will be what gives you your sense of self.** If that's what your love does for you, and that's what keeps you in it, it's time to leave until you can fill yourself with love first.

EVERYTHING IN YOUR LIFE IS FEEDBACK

THE UNIVERSE IS CONTINUOUSLY morphing in compilations of our own creation mixed with the creations of others (other people, a higher being, whatever you believe). This accounts for the discord and harmony we are perpetually affected by. The challenge it poses is being able to find the equilibrium between being adamant and determined with your own journey and manifestation while also being conscious and nonresistant to the moments of discord that come in the interim.

It is the root of our conflict and suffering, but also of the most incredible creation and experience we have. We are cultures and a people because we have been able to co-create for so long, and whether you believe so or not, we are responsible, at least partially, for all that is. I am speaking literally, but I also mean metaphysically. Thoughts are wavelengths, just the same as tangible wavelengths such as voice is–it's just that we can physically experience the latter. Thoughts are also vibrational frequencies, much like all other matter. Without a physical presence, the physical around us wouldn't exist. Wavelengths need to be touched by something to be comprehensible. Essentially, we are spiritual beings in a physical world, adapting to the needs that our souls require to grow.

What's more is that just as your life is within your control (even the aspects you think are the furthest from it) you must realize that everything has meaning and nothing is by chance. Signs and messages are surrounding you, you're just not paying attention. If I may be so bold as to declare my belief in a higher being, (although I do respect that others opinions may vary), I think that said being is intertwining with your greater spirit and energy and assisting through the process of growth and the journey of discovery. There is a meaning behind every single thing that happens in your life. Everything is a sign or message, and everybody is a messenger. My dad used to tell me growing up: "everything is feedback." It is. Everything in your life you have brought to it, and I know it would seem ridiculous that you could ever bring forth tragedy and misery into your life, but you have and it's absolutely crucial that you realize this. Your life changes the day you decide it should. You are happy the day you decide you will be, or that you will take the necessary steps to facilitate it.

You must let go of your physical, egotistical understanding of yourself, and replace it with the idea that you are just being. When you can tune into the stillness and calmness inside you, you can release yourself of your need to create yourself, and you can trust the greater that understands. Your mind is nothing but electric currents zapping back and forth making sure you keep breathing, your heart keeps going and you are staying alive. It does not have the capability to process things that are of the spiritual nature like the heart and soul can. Because real creation isn't just in what we mindlessly do and think about, it's what we feel and embrace and perpetuate with all of our senses. Yes, thoughts create, but feelings? They're responsible for the life you live even now.

WHAT YOUR FUTURE SELF WOULD TELL YOU NOW

YOU KNOW THE ADAGE, that you should really only concern yourself with things that will matter a few years down the line. If you can imagine what you would have done 5 years ago if the you that you are now were there, you can assume that your future self will want to give your present self some similar advice. That being:

1. Make time for the things that make you happy. Your baseline of happiness will fluctuate with major life changes, but will eventually return to whatever is your

norm. For example, after your needs are taken care of, a plethora of extra money won't really aide your innate happiness. You have to work on the baseline. That's best done by the little, everyday things that make you feel good. They seem small and insignificant and like they won't matter in the end, but they will, and they do, because what matters in the end is that you're happy right now.

2. Don't concern yourself with petty things that upset you, like associating with friends who only serve to make you feel bad about yourself, worrying largely what other people will think to the point of making your own decisions based on those opinions. Criticism is important for the growing process, but at the end of the day, you have to be able to differentiate

between what will help you and what is only negativity aimed to hurt you.

3. Have a little more faith that the universe has it figured out. That's the biggest thing that strikes me when I think about what I wish I knew five years ago. I can see now how many little, insignificant things were signs and callings and how I was led in directions I was completely opposed to and how I wasted my time and energy being opposed when the universe knew what was right for me. Today, I couldn't be happier or more thankful that I didn't get a lot of what I wanted 5 years ago.

4. Let yourself let go of what keeps you all pretzeled up inside. Easier said than done, I know, I know. But I know I wish I could have told myself that I was literally wasting my time being worried about things that worrying could not change.

Things will, without exception, work out how they are supposed to, and although it's a cliché, you have to understand how true it is. You also have to trust it.

5. Don't let anybody else dictate how you feel about yourself or what you do with your life. You are not a democracy. Nobody else gets a vote. Taking the opinions of others into consideration and letting them dictate your decision are two completely different animals, and you have to understand how to do the former without the latter. Nobody has to live in your body or live your life, so make decisions for your own sake.

6. Approach things from your best self. I think we can all recall times we wish we wouldn't have been so brash, harsh, cruel, passive... I could go on and on. When tough situations arise, I think we have

tendencies to react very instinctively and that doesn't always bring forth the most flattering versions of us. Especially when the things being dealt with are difficult and personal. We often make situations worse when if we would have just put in a little effort to be a bigger person, we could have seen a different outcome.

7. Focus on what does, and what will, matter: the things you won't always have. You will not have all of your family members around forever. You may not be in close proximity to a friend a few years down the line. You will never be right where you are again, and you will look back and wish you took advantage of everything right now has to offer.

24 THINGS YOU SHOULDN'T HAVE TO MAKE EXCUSES FOR

1. **Momentary discrepancies in your calm and cool demeanor.** We all lose it a little now and again. Actually, many of us lose it more than just a little. You don't need to make excuses for going through a rough patch. You are entitled to your feelings, and you are allowed to be honest about them. You need not defend yourself with reasons you could be disinterested or struggling if they aren't the truth. Unless, of course, you aren't comfortable with

exposing something personal, in which case saying so would be appropriate.

2. **Needing time to yourself, or not wanting to talk to someone.** It does not necessarily mean you are completely anti-social or that you hate the person in question. Sometimes we just need to be left alone to collect our thoughts, work through some things, deprogram and reprogram and do a little self-modulating.

3. **What makes you successful.** In my opinion, everyone needs to define what they are going to measure their success by and stick to it. If you want to do so by traditional means like wealth or affluence, so be it. If you'd rather gauge how successful you are by how much you have helped other people, or how much you

enjoy each day, that is just as legitimate, if not more so.

4. **Mental illness.** People tend to deny that they are struggling with a legitimate mental illness, probably because of the stigmas attached, or they deflect the idea by excuses along the lines of, well, I went through a difficult phase, or it runs in my family. You aren't at fault for having an illness. You don't need anything to justify why you have it, either.

5. **What your significant other does or doesn't do.** Love will not pay the bills. But paid bills will not give you love, and if you're more concerned about true, unconditional love than a trust fund, that is all you need to seek. We're confronted with so many questions when we bring up a new prospective significant other: what

do they do? Where did they go to school? Are they wealthy? What do they look like? What do their parents do? It doesn't matter. You don't need to make excuses for why they did or didn't attend school and where, or where they work just because someone would look down on it.

6. **What your significant other or the object of your affection looks like.** Similarly, whether or not your boo is tattooed, pierced, dressed like a dirty hippie or in New York's finest, you should just dismiss the reactions people will have and don't ever succumb by saying things along the lines of: "they look better when they clean up." It's just insulting to the person and what's more is that it is nothing that you need to make excuses for.

7. **How you choose to dress, groom and present yourself.** If nobody else has to live in your body, nobody else gets a say or a valid opinion on what you choose to do with it. This goes both ways: you are free to dress as up or down as is acceptable for your workplace and conducive to your lifestyle and happiness.

8. **What you spend your money on.** Clothes and dinners out? Your choice. You will most likely be subject to advice on how you should save and invest and cut corners regardless of how you spend your money, but you know what? That advice is solid and should be considered. But you know what else? You do not have to take it unless you want to. If it is your money and you have earned it, you are free to do as you please.

9. **If you actually do want to get married young, have children and be a quintessential housewife or be a working husband with a wife that stays home.** The trend tends to be leaning toward taking a period of time for self-discovery and putting off family and children, and of course, that women should work. While all of that is absolutely fantastic, if you decide it's not for you, that's perfectly fine too. Note: I'm not saying I'm necessarily of one opinion or the other, because I think every woman is different and what will make her happy/what will work best for her logistically differs greatly.

10. **...Or if you never want to do any of those things and disagree with them wholeheartedly.** Equally as valid.

11. **Who you have sex with and how often.** There is no rule as to how many sexual partners you can have and to what extent you can be involved with them before you are a leper of society. Those "rules" and people being "sluts" or "man-whores" is all just nonsense. Be safe. Take care of yourself. Respect your partner. Do not apologize for a healthy sex life.

12. **The fact that you made mistakes in the past, or that you may not have been the greatest person at one point.** I know I wasn't. Sometimes I'm still not. You don't have to be sorry about these things, because you never have to be sorry for what you innately are, in this case: human. You show me someone who thinks they are flawless and I'll show you a deluded individual.

13. **If you don't have a relationship with your parents or family members.** People will always advise that you make peace and rekindle relationships, and understandably so. A strong familial support system is fantastic if you have it. But here's the thing: sometimes distancing yourself from people is the best thing you can do. You can make a family of your own choosing. Sometimes the people we are genetically related to happen to be incapable of loving us and their presence in our lives isn't worth it. It's for you to judge.

14. **The size of your pants.** You need not defend yourself with "real women are curvy" or I'm beautiful or handsome and it doesn't matter what size my pants are. Your pants just are whatever size they are.

Don't categorize your attractiveness and then defend it for not being ideal.

15. **Your singledom.** You don't need to be single because you are finishing school or you're taking time for yourself or you are completely against the institution of marriage... you can be single just because you are.

16. **If you want to binge on junk food or be a strict vegan.** It's your body and you can fuel it as you please, just as you will live with the consequences of how you do so.

17. **That you left someone.** I know breakups tend to be more difficult on the receiving end, but it's equally crappy to be the one leaving because you are most likely going to have a lot of guilt and blame placed on you. It's not to say that you shouldn't be as

respectful about it as possible, but it is to say that if you want to go, you need no other excuse than that.

18. **The books you like.** Whether you spend your free time reading Deepak Chopra or *Twilight*, it doesn't matter. You don't have to explain how and why you only read it for the great plot or excellent writing or because everybody told you you had to.

19. **That you like Miley Cyrus' new song.** Or whatever top 40 music is "uncool" to listen to but you dig anyway and sass your way down the street to.

20. **How many bars and clubs you go to or if you've never had a drink in your life.** There is this overwhelming stigma that the only "cool" place to be is the bar, and it's just not so. It implies that drinking is the best way to enjoy yourself and that is

simply not the case for everybody. But at the same time, you should never feel embarrassed or ashamed of your affinity to go to the bar and drink. Either which way you roll, you do not owe anyone an excuse.

21. **Why you're awesome and doing so well.** So often we downplay the good things in our lives by saying *oh, well, it wasn't always this way...* or *oh, it's only because of this...* Yes you do so to be tasteful, and that's understandable, but at least know in your own mind that, yes, you did get your life together, and you are doing really well, and you do not need to belittle yourself so other people won't judge you for being aware of your awesomeness.

22. **If you choose to leave your job to pursue a dream or you choose to stay**

because it's what makes the most sense for you. Everybody likes to tell everybody else when to stay and when to go, and the reality is that sometimes going after a dream in lieu of a stable job weighs so heavily on the risks that the possibility of success just isn't the most responsible gamble to make.

23. **Same goes for a partner.** I am not referring to situations where partners are abusive or there are serious issues that cannot be ignored. I mean that aside from those dire situations, you do not ever have to explain why you are choosing a long-distance relationship while everybody is shaking their heads that it won't work or why you're rekindling things with the former flame you never quite entirely put out and they're having the same reactions.

24. **Having a broken heart, in more ways than just being romantically jaded.** It's as though the idea of being broken over someone somehow makes you pathetic and sad. Really, it means you cared about someone very much, and that you are just going through one of the many phases of human life. Heartbreak, in every terrible form it comes in, is a universal experience, and some people will find themselves irritated that you can't just simply move on because they are recalling the time they couldn't do so themselves. Don't let that make you feel as though your feelings are invalid–because fighting them is like trying to put out fire with gasoline.

20 TRUTHS THAT CAN CHANGE EVERYTHING

1. **You can easily define your life with your fears.** Don't underestimate the power of what you are afraid of. It is the root of much of existence as we know it. You can neglect your full potential because of being afraid. Know that it is nothing more than a mind game. Danger is real. Heartache is real. Fear is not. It's a story we tell ourselves.

2. **The important questions usually can't be answered.** There are many questions that people have tried to answer for

thousands of years, but to no avail. Or at least not one that is universally agreed upon. The things that matter usually don't have concise and easily attainable answers. The mystery is part of the magic.

3. **Much of your suffering is rooted in attachment and expectation.** Learn to jive with the ebb and flow of things. The most beautiful thing I have learned, through countless examples in my own life and observations in the lives of others, is that very often when things don't work out the way you want them to, you hold onto what you think should be because you see no alternative. That alternative is right around the corner. Just wait for it.

4. **If you want meaning in your life, learn to apply it.** There is no universal meaning

for life. It is, simply, what you make it. So make it what you want. There is nobody else who should dictate what your meaning is, so it's up to you to apply it. I suggest applying it to the beautiful, everyday things that keep you going. The things you may overlook, but you'd be lost without: the things that really matter most.

5. **Being kind is more powerful than you probably realize.** You will be amazed at how many people, hearts and opportunities open up when you open your heart to them. It's a tricky business, kindness, because we live in a world rampant with cruelty, and some may trickle in. Don't let it close you.

6. **Happiness requires the ability to embrace uncertainty.** Happiness has everything to do with just living for

today–something most of us are slow to master, if at all. People think that they'll be happy once they have this thing or that thing, or at the very least, that they know love and success and wonderful things are coming. It's like we need something to make today's suffering worth it. But here's the thing: tomorrow may never come. Love and success and wonderful things may never come, or they may, and they may leave just as quickly. Nothing is certain but what you have today, so it's the only logical thing to base your happiness on.

7. **"Eternal silence is always at hand."** If you have something to do or say, now is the time. You may not always have the opportunity to say what you think or feel. You may not always have the opportunity

to tell somebody that you love them. I know there are a dozen reasons you would rather not, but there's only one reason to do so if you feel compelled to: you may not have another chance.

8. **Life will rarely look like what you thought it would.** Some things will be worse, some will be better than you ever could have imagined...and some will just be different. Many grandiose visions that we have never come to pass, so learn to release them. Spending everyday comparing your reality to the ideas you had in your head will always leave you feeling shortchanged.

9. **"This too shall pass."** The pain will pass, but so will the other things that you may not always have around to enjoy. It's just a

simple reminder that everything is fleeting and temporary.

10. **It is always the little things.** This has a lot to do with the concept of your baseline of happiness, something I've written about before. Your overall level of contentment will briefly fluctuate with great successes or major tragedies. You will eventually return to your baseline. To change that, you must fill your everyday life with the little things that make you happy. In retrospect, you will most often find, that the things you most remember and look back on most fondly are little, and would otherwise seem insignificant.

11. **If you don't go after it, you'll never have it.** If you never ask, the answer will always be no. All you need is a few seconds of courage. It's scary when your

pride is at stake, and you're afraid of losing someone or damaging your reputation. But if you feel something is so inherently true and you are otherwise compelled to say so but are withheld by your fears, take that step. Even if it doesn't go the way you wanted, you can at least cross one other avenue off your list of possibilities.

12. **Consider trying to adopt some qualities of the person you'd like to fall in love with.** By that I mean, love yourself first. You should always be your own person, I don't mean to say that you should base your own self around someone else, I just mean to propose another way to learn to love yourself. Very often, the qualities that we would ideally like in a partner are the ones that

we wish we had ourselves. Don't wait for someone else to complete you.

13. **What you think, you become.** It's an ancient principle, but it is one of the things I have found to be most true. Change your mindset, change your life.

14. **Equal does not have to mean the same: embrace and respect your differences.** Being human is all you need to be eligible for equality. You need not prove yourself as being "the same" as someone else to feel worthy of equality. You deserve it, as does everybody else, just because you are.

15. **When things least look like they are going to change, they usually do.** There's only one way up from rock bottom, right? When things seem absolutely hopeless and you've all but given up, something beautiful and little

and miraculous usually shows up and leads you to the revelation you've been waiting for.

16. **Never cease to be thankful.** Imagine if someone less privileged than you lived your life with you for a day. Imagine how grateful some people would be to have food in the refrigerator and a computer or fancy phone to be reading this on... lest we forget just the privilege to be able to read.

17. **Mind over matter.** 10% what happens, 90% how you react. Always.

18. **There is an atlas in your gut.** Listen to it. Those little voices and feelings are not to be ignored. The tricky thing, though, is that they're just that: little. Easy to brush off and ignore. So often arriving in a swamp of other "nonsensical" thoughts

and feelings. Believe me, it's worth your time to learn to differentiate what your gut feeling is. It will serve you in ways beyond what you can imagine.

19. **Always consider what you would do if money were no object in your life.** We are controlled by our need for money. It can be very difficult to differentiate what you want from your life with what you need simply because in our society you need money to survive. It may not always be practical, but it will always be beneficial to consider what we'd do with our lives if we were just here to be, and all our needs were taken care of. It will help you to define yourself for who you are, not what you are conditioned to be.

20. **You usually know what the right thing to do is.** It's just a matter of having the courage to do it. More often than not, you do have the answer. It's just a matter of having the courage to do what you know you should.

HOW TO LET GO

1. **Change your inner monologue.** You know the stories we tell ourselves throughout the day? How we pretend we are this and that and the other thing? How we imagine what our every move would look like if that one special person were with us? You have to change that story to reflect the truth. They aren't there. They aren't going to be.

2. **Don't pick and choose what parts of the person or relationship you let go of.** You will never forget if you are always reminding yourself. You are not doing

yourself any favors by thinking about all the wonderful times you had together. You can't decide to let go of someone and hold on to their memory. To do this right, it's an all-or-nothing deal.

3. **Change your plans.** I think that's what we tend to cry about more than anything: everything we could have had and could have been with that person. All those plans you had to travel and love each other and have babies together, and how sad it is that they're all done now. Just because one person is gone does not mean that your whole life is too. You can keep the plans themselves if you'd like, just change who you assumed they'd be with.

4. **Dignify yourself.** Prior to the letting go phase, you were (are) most likely in the exhaust-all-options-possible phase. You

have put your pride aside, you laid it all on the table. You were brutally honest with yourself and with them... but to no avail. Worse, if you feel your dignity was taken from you rather than you giving it up, learn to re-dignify yourself. Walk away with your head up high. Make them fuel to your fire. Burn through it. See where it gets you. The fuel will run out, but not before you're in a much better place.

5. **Accept that, at least for the time being, even if you do still love them, you are choosing to move on anyway.** Just because you love someone does not mean you should be with them, and vice versa. You can love someone and be broken up about them and that can be part of your story. It can stand alone.

Acceptance does not necessarily mean being happy about something... it just means recognizing it for what it is and letting it be that way.

6. **Understand that this is not a unique situation, and that virtually everybody has dealt with this to a lesser or greater extent than you have.** Think of the people who have been seriously wronged, cheated on, left with a family, left for another family, left to look at their children each day and know that they will always have to have that person in their lives because of their children. Sometimes people are inescapable. Be grateful for the ability to completely let them go if you have it.

7. **Rearrange.** Changes in life require some rearranging. A little travelling, a little

redecorating, a new haircut, a change of summer plans, weekend plans, you know how it goes. When your personal life undergoes a major change, but nothing else does, the absence becomes much clearer.

INSIGHTS TO GET YOU THROUGH LIFE

DRINK WATER AND PAY the bills and love people. Paint, make art, make love, make lists, make whatever the hell you want. Travel on the weekends and dress for the weather. See movies and go out to eat and stay in touch with friends and wear clothes just because you like them. Know that there is a time to work, a time to rest, a time to be sure and a time to choose: all of which will arrive and pass as you are ready. Become a proponent of peace. Love those who don't love you. You don't have to agree, but you must tolerate and respect, even if such courtesies are not given

169

to you. Most of all, never let anybody shame you for living your truth. Let your soul out. Experience and immerse yourself in the only thing you really have–right now.

— **The best and most transformative kind of love,** the real, genuine, love-you-so-much-it-hurt-and-changes-me-at-my-core-kind-of-love is a striking bliss mixed with the reality of someone unveiling who you really are–and the realization that some parts may not be pretty. We can get so ugly in so many ways after this happens. This kind of love, the kind that reaches into you and touches you at every level that anything undealt with rises is sometimes painful, sometimes excruciating, sometimes all effed up but always wonderful, undeniable and somehow, beautiful.

Don't destroy yourself over this kind of love, create yourself.

— **You can fill yourself with guilt, shame and remorse** that you didn't choose a different path. That you didn't put your best self forward. That you weren't better. But it's pointless, and will deprive you of enjoying today. So choose to love and accept yourself–the good, bad and the ugly. Love yourself the way you want to love someone else, the way you hope they would love you: for all your little quirks and flaws. You do not have to be perfect to be loved. Life does not have to be perfect to be absolutely wonderful–it has not and will never be.

— **The future has an ancient heart.** Cheryl Strayed once said that in an advice column and it always stuck with me. Your life is no accident. Things don't come out of nowhere. You will be perplexed but amazed at where life takes you, and in retrospect, all the little twists and turns in the story will make sense. Logic will rarely get you anywhere extraordinary. Love is not logical. Miracles are not logical. Signs and messages and signals are everywhere if you just pay attention. They have been there for all your life, and as the years unfold, you will put the pieces together and see how what preceded prepared you for now.

— **You will always be in equilibrium** between doing what you want to now and what will be best for the long term. But you have to learn to live in the grey space sometimes. Learn to use your heart and head in tandem, but always in that order. Sometimes your passions and what brings your income in don't overlap. That's okay. Life rarely comes neatly packaged. At some point, you probably won't know whether to stay or to go–from your job, relationship, home. You won't be sure whether or not you should give up or keep trying. That's also okay. You don't have to know. Life is never clearly black and white, it's most often a masterpiece of greys that make it dynamic and complex and interesting. You shouldn't want it any other way. Uncertainty is nothing to run from. It keeps you guessing, trying different things and going down paths you wouldn't have otherwise. Be patient.

— **People are going to dislike you regardless** of how beautiful and kind and successful you are. The idea that you will one day reach a point where everybody likes you is absolutely delusional. These people, unfortunately, are being true to themselves by being aware that they don't like you. A natural part of being human is conflicting tastes and opinions, and sometimes that applies to people. It is their problem if they choose to act on it. It is your problem if you let it affect you. Otherwise, it is nothing. It is noise. It is irrelevant because the negative opinions of others will not affect how the people worth being in your life will feel about you. That is what I've found that concerns people most, because we don't really care what strangers or acquaintances think, they aren't in our lives that much. It's the threat of what those opinions can do to what and who is.

— **We build our own cages** and live within them because we think they will keep us safe. Some of us are internal about it but I think in many ways that safety net is legitimate and physical. I think we see something that threatens our being, confidence, any sense of knowing that we're okay — and we set up a bar. We know to not go there again. But when we start living within that cage, and decorating its steel bars with pretty little flowers, we're brainwashed into thinking that it's the real, free universe. That's the stuff of breakdowns. We stop building cages and start digging graves. Free yourself from the confines that bind you. Maybe you built steel bars around your heart because you thought they had to be there. You wanted to protect yourself from being hurt so badly again. Take them down. Walk out. This may be physical or it may be metaphorical. But either way, know that there's nothing worse than not experiencing life for the fear of what it may bring.

— **There is no wrong way to live.** You can love who you love. No excuses or justifications required. You need not feel guilty or have to explain your choices to anybody if you don't feel the need to. It is your body and if it leads you to your mistakes, then so be it. They are your lessons to learn, nobody else's. Your mistakes are yours to make. Your successes and glories are yours to embrace. It is greater to be free and to make mistakes than to be caged and unable to learn and experience for yourself.

— **"Tomorrow" will never come.** You will always be waiting for tomorrow if you don't start living for today. You will always be waiting for the next big thing to come: the job, the degree, the partner, the house, the time to travel, the money, I could go on. Once you get into the mindset of perpetually waiting, you'll also fall into the habit of not being okay with things as they are. Because more likely than not, you will get most of those things, and when they come, you won't enjoy hem because you will only be looking forward to the next thing. You may want to retaliate with, well, there's nothing to be happy about now, but you have to learn to make it for yourself. You have to learn to see it. You have to learn to be grateful and gracious and enjoy the very simple things. You cannot expect life to deliver to you what you feel you deserve. Because everybody deserves the best and not everybody gets it handed to them, so many times, you have to go and get it yourself.

WHEN TO LET GO AND WHEN TO TRY HARDER

EVENTUALLY, WE ALL REACH the crossroad of moving on or trying harder. While it's difficult to go either way, the decision is what is more perplexing. Sometimes you can't just let things be, and other times things really do just have to work themselves out. But how do we know the difference?

Well, we often don't, and that's the most important part. The process of figuring out what we can't change and when it's time to move on is the actual process of doing so. Because while you can't change things when they are largely the decisions of others, your actions can change the minds of those people. How do you know when the universe will work it out and how do you know when it's time for you to start ironing out the kinks? You don't until you've tried.

It's time to move on when you have tried to change things, but to no avail. It's time to let the higher being or whatever it is you do or don't believe in figure things out– and have faith in the funny little way that life tends to bring and take what we need at just the right times. But regardless of where you are in the journey, you have to keep trying until there is no other option. And that's what's going to be so incredible and humbling about when you finally realize it's time to let go. Because you've been down to your knees and you don't have anything more to give. That is what is going to bring you to a place of having something to let go of. It's only then that the universe will take over. Trust it. Do it. You will find the "wisdom to know the difference" at the end.

8 THINGS YOU GAIN WHEN YOU LOSE SOMEONE

1. **The starting revelation** of just how much you appreciate the people in your life, which is sadly most noticeable when there is a gaping hole.

2. **Fuel to move you forward.** Few things are more devastating than a nasty breakup or losing a loved one; most of us are filled and teeming with negative energy. Channel it, change it and use it to your advantage.

3. **A clean slate.** Whether you want to acknowledge it or not, your life has changed incredibly. You can now decide what you fill the person's absence with.

4. **A rediscovered understanding/sense of self.** You're either contemplating why and how they could have left you or the things you wish you would or wouldn't have done when they were still around. Regardless, an excellent (though heartbreaking) means of self-reflection.

5. **Inspiration.** To write or compose or take on any new endeavor in your life. Just listen to love songs and books and novels and poems... the most common theme? Unrequited or lost love or loved ones and the guilt, regret, despair and eventual realization and enlightenment that follows.

6. **The crucifixion before the resurrection.** I've used this phrase many times before, but I'm saying it again because I do honestly believe that to really find enlightenment you must lose something.

7. **The discovery of how powerful your resilience can be.**

8. **Eventually, a deeper understanding** of the interesting and intricate ways life blindsides you but leads you somewhere better, even when it least seems like that's the case.

7 Things You May Be Letting Pass You By

THIS IS INTENDED TO be in the context of what you're missing when you're not living in the "here and now": the elusive state of being that we're all lectured on, told tales about the greatness of and yet can rarely seem to accomplish. Here, my friends, are some ideas that may aide you on that journey. Seven things you may miss if you don't live in the moment:

1. **The love that people are trying to give you. It doesn't manifest itself and wait around until you're ready to receive it. Take it today or leave it forever.**

People love you. They really, honestly do. It seems like we all spend half of our time painstakingly searching for this great life-changing love when really, love is right in front of our noses. The problem, however, is that as with all things in life, it doesn't usually look or feel like we thought it would. It can be jaded and suppressed, familial and fleeting, temporary and mind-blowing, there when we never expected and vice versa.

2. **The accomplished goals, dreams that were sought and conquered, challenges that are no longer plaguing you: these are the days you once fantasized about.**

The things you worked so hard to have now that seemed like the answer to your woes a year ago (or further back). We never actually get to enjoy the things we're after because once they're here we're after something else.

3. **The understated beauty in the art of just being.**

The way your body is functioning to keep you alive in tandem with the consciousness you experience, the thoughts you're capable of having, the feelings that can overwhelm you, it's like our whole lives are foreign travels and we're only fooled into thinking we're not around the corner from another new discovery.

4. **That "forever" is a million little "nows."**

You've probably heard that idea phrased different ways, but the principle is the same. Once you feel loved and have great things in your life finally, the next phase is the how do I keep this for as long as I can mentality. It's almost like a subconscious retaliation to the fact that we're attaching ourselves to things that we cannot, in fact, take with us. If you want something that will last forever, or if you want to live out the "forever" you promised someone else–realize that this is just another piece of that puzzle.

5. Doors that are open today that may close tomorrow–and never re-open.

What right now has to offer. Whether it seems like it or not, there are opportunities everywhere, you just have to look for them and be willing to see them for what they are:

the difficulties they may bring and all. The most promising opportunities are the ones that are present right now... not the ones you'll be eternally searching for. And these are the stepping-stones to getting to them anyway.

6. **Your youth: with every second, another drop of it trickles away.**

Regardless of how young you are in years, you are still as young as you'll ever be again. With youth comes a lot of things that are important to aiding the human condition: wonder for today and hope for tomorrow. Don't let that slip by you. Remember when you were a kid and you were dying to drive a car and shave your face/legs and buy food and do other grown-up things? They're not as fun when they're responsibilities.

7. **What you are capable of doing and creating because of who you are and where you are right now. These traits and circumstances of yours will never be exactly the same again. Much like love, you can either utilize them or let them pass you by.**

What you are capable of creating right now is something that you may never and will probably never be able to replicate. At this very second, your mind and heart are at a place in the journey that they will never return to. This "life" business is a constant evolution, and if you don't pull art and love and writing and everything else that's beautiful out of yourself it will simply pass and dissolve. But when you take it out, and write it down, or give it to someone else or express it in one way or another, it remains. And the residue of the dissolution doesn't build into walls of closedness and darkness that too many of us know.

WHAT THEY'RE REALLY LOOKING FOR IN A RELATIONSHIP

I KEEP SEEING ALL of these articles and messages and "concrete ideas" about what men and women have to do to be date-able. These things tend to be rather gender-oriented, usually specific to the writer's pet-peeves and generally present a negative way of thinking of yourself in the context of wanting to be in a relationship. Now, of course, sweeping generalizations for the entire population of human beings will inevitably yield falsehoods for some people, and I respect and understand that, just as I expect that you understand it would be absolutely impossible for me to talk about every single thing every person was looking for in a relationship… ever. I merely mean to discuss what most people are really after. The things that matter. This does not apply to every kind of relationship, of course. Some people are just looking for someone to have sex with, maybe a short-term fling, maybe a forever-deal. But regardless, here are some simple things that we can't forget in the vortex of everything we "should" and "shouldn't" be:

1. I used the pronoun "they" in the headline because here's the deal: some people like women and some people like men and some people like both and some people like neither. Beyond that, being a "man" and a "woman" are really societally contrived ideas that few people flawlessly fall into–not without a

little personal turmoil, anyway. So the idea of what men want and what women want is largely false by the fact that sex and gender is not so simply divided. You can be as much of a man or as much of a woman or as much of neither or as much of both as you damn well please and I promise you, there will be someone out there who is looking for just what you are. Sounds a bit idealistic? You're feeling a little unsure? Give it time, my friend. We're all non-believers until it happens to us.

2. We are all looking for the X factor, the magic, the unexplainable-don't-know-why-you-drive-me-crazy-with-love-but-you-do factor. We are no longer following in our ancestors' footsteps of marrying the first person we date or settling down because it's expected.

Some people find this earlier than others, and happen to fall into the preconceived conventions of what life should look like and hey, good for you, I'm happy for you. But for most of us, it takes time to work out our own issues, get a grasp on this "loving ourselves" business and then sift through people until we finally find the right one. But the most important thing about this is that sometimes, it just isn't there, and you'll usually be conflicted about it because it will seem as though everything else about this person is perfect except that gut feeling just isn't coming forth. If someone leaves you over this, don't shower yourself in a perpetual hate bath of why you're not good enough. They are doing you a favor. I cannot say that intently enough.

3. People want someone they can trust. Someone who will listen to them, who will talk with them, who will enjoy the often mundane day-to-day activities that inevitably come with a relationship. Someone who will be kind, understanding, willing to accept an imperfect person, and to work on things when they inevitably need to be worked on. This is the kind of person that most people take the most pride and assurance in being in a relationship with. It is more important than how gorgeous you are. It is more important than how much money you make. It is more important than the things that are fleeting.

4. Above all else, people want to love and be loved. To be accepted for who they are and not who they may one day be.

People want to be someone that rearranges how a person thinks their story will unfold rather than fit into the preconceived character that they had imagined. There is a certain sense of security that comes with someone saying you can tell me anything and you know it's true. Someone proclaiming that they love you not in spite of all your little embarrassing quirks you tried to hide but because of them. These things are not as complicated as people make them out to be. Because what people want out of a relationship is to have something in their lives that makes them happy... whatever "happy" means to them.

FOR WHEN YOU'RE HATING HOW YOU LOOK...

1. I would venture to say that perpetual contentment with anything in life is what's abnormal. You do not have to like how you look at all times. It's almost worse to force yourself into doing that because honestly, as we all know, forcing emotions to either be there or go away never works. If you're having a "bad body" day (meaning you don't like how you look, your body itself is never "bad") just say, okay, I'm feeling a little crappy about this today, but so are a million other people, and it will pass eventually.

2. Figure out if this is your genuine opinion or if you're more concerned with how "people" will perceive you. This "people" demon that haunts us is very interesting, because we all seem to be very concerned about this group of faceless monsters who decide who we are based on what we fear we're projecting to others. It's crazy if you think about it. Think of someone who loves you, someone whose opinion matters... they're a person, aren't they? So I'd venture to assume that they fall under the "people" category, right? ... Meaning that not all "people" think these terrible things of you. When you start putting faces to this "people" fear, you'll start to realize that it's mostly a projection of your own opinions.

3. If the best thing about you is how you look, I feel compelled to say that it's time

you do a bit of soul-searching. The friends who are worth being friends with aren't going to care what you look like if they love you for something more than that. Focus on the "more than that" that I promise you other people see. These are the traits that are most innately "you." Things that don't rely on your outer appearance. Things that will not fade with time, but rather, grow.

4. There is always an element of attraction that is vital for any relationship, but do you know what's more important than that? Loving someone for reasons other than that. You would be inspired by how many men and women honestly aren't as concerned about how physically beautiful you are as much as you make them laugh, and feel loved, and have things in common, and enjoy nights out together,

and talk for hours about nothing and everything. That's where real love derives.

5. Sometimes it is time to make a change. This probably isn't what you were expecting, but hear me out. The truth is sometimes we do gain weight and sometimes we lose it and we are supposed to fluctuate. We shouldn't, however, let it get out of control to the point where we are physically incapable of doing things we once loved, are suffering from medical issues, etc. Part of "loving yourself" is being honest with yourself about when it's time to make a change, and not for the sake of appeasing others or the little gremlins in your head.

6. If you ever need a quick pick-me-up in this department, think about or write down what your body lets you do, not what it prohibits you from. My list

consists of things like hugging my little brother, allowing me to think and write and express what I'm most passionate about, to enjoy foods that I love, to smell spring days and move around and travel. Your body is a vessel for your experience, and you will be trapped until you realize that what the vessel looks like is not as important as what it can do.

8 TRUTHS ABOUT WHO YOU REALLY ARE

1. We traditionally use jobs, genders, roles in relationships, etc. to define who we are, but we realize after those jobs are lost, gender roles fail and relationships deteriorate that if we do so, we are lost when they are. Your "true self" cannot be lost, and thus, these are not valid ways of defining who you are.

2. You are a constant evolution, who you are is not static, and you have to learn to be okay with that.

3. This means to act on what you think and feel at any given moment. To make your own decisions based on what you feel compelled toward.

4. It is so difficult largely because part of the human condition is fearing being isolated, failing, the unknown, etc. and all of these issues will come into play readily if you are genuinely being yourself.

5. This is because you are paving a way of life that nobody else has before. There can be similarities, but never exactness. Because, as simply as I can put it, there is nobody who has your exact state of consciousness.

6. But we are fooled into thinking that once we just decide to "be ourselves" that we will be happy and carefree, and thus we

retreat to following the crowd when that doesn't come to pass.

7. And while in that confused state, we rely on constants in our lives to define us: I am a sister, a writer, a singer, and that's what makes me who I am is the kind of nonsense we tell ourselves. Because while it is what we choose to be each day because we love it, we can always choose differently. Those things can be gone tomorrow either by choice or circumstance.

8. So we have to evaluate ourselves on the level of who we are statically. What part of us does not change? Simply, our consciousness. Our state of being. And to be ourselves we have to follow what that person decides each day and be who that person wants to be in each moment and not get caught in expectations or titles or labels or roles that provide false comfort.

THE TRUTH ABOUT THE PEOPLE WE HATE

I THINK ONE OF the most difficult things we can ever master is genuinely accepting people for who they are, even when we inherently disagree with it. Even when we are so passionately in disagreement with what they believe or who they are, we still respect and love them because they are worthy of that, just as we are. This is coming in light of reports that a Catholic cardinal referred to gay people as "faggots" while being interviewed. What's interesting, though, is that while there is a decent amount of backlash, it's nothing incredible or abnormal... because we're used to this. We've come to expect this kind of degrading treatment and hate culture because it surrounds us... especially on the internet.

What's so difficult is that we want to correct what we think is wrong when "right" and "wrong" are subjective. But accepting that fact leaves us in a limbo of uncertainty. We've placed meaning on what we believe is right and wrong; it's what we use to formulate opinions about ourselves. Even if it leaves you a bit unsteady, it's absolutely crucial to realize that all lives are valid, even if they are, by our standards, wrong and hateful.

We go on violently disagreeing over religion and what the truth of the universe is, literally killing one another over who knows the real truth and who should be killed because they don't when nobody knows for certain. We only believe we do.

Because the truth of the matter is that if you compare the lives of those who are deeply religious, and those who are not, I imagine you'll come to find that they are very similar. Not necessarily by the way they practice spirituality, but the gauge of "goodness" in the sense of being loving, kind, accepting, etc. If anything, what history has taught us is that those who are most inherently religious lean more toward the opposite end of the goodness spectrum than those who aren't. More wars have been waged over religion than anything else.

It's ironic, frankly, because religion is supposed to be the practice with which we find solace and understanding; love and acceptance for our own lives and others, and understanding of our reason and purpose here on Earth. But when we come to believe things so inherently that we cannot open our minds to the beliefs of others, we falsely start to believe that in some way, we're above them.

The most difficult thing that we may need to come to understand is that all life is sacred, and not in the necessarily religiously-affiliated sense. People are worthy of love and acceptance even when their lives are not like your own. People deserve love and marriage and the right to believe what they want. Just because they don't believe what you do is no reason for name-calling or other such discrimination.

The spectrum of "right and wrong" is completely subjective and entirely up to interpretation. The people and environment around you may completely convince you that you are correct and that the rest of the world is wrong, and that's something that we often take great console in...knowing what we're